How To Stop Debt-Collecting Agencies From Destroying Your Credit Score

SVW Rorie

Introduction

So, let me guess: you recently looked at your FICO score and don't like what you are seeing.

You went online to see what that score means and realized that you belong in the "not good" category or worse.

You know what that means. It means that the best lenders in the country won't lend you even one dollar of their money. They consider you a "risky borrower." Providian Financial used to have another term for someone in your shoes. They used to call you part of the "unbanked market." Distasteful, I know.

But it gets worse. Your creditors have sold off your previous debts to collectors. And no, these collectors are not carrying baseball bats and knocking on your door to demand payment. But they are constantly harassing you with all kinds of threats. They're even threatening to report your debts to credit bureaus.

With your current credit score, you know what an added negative on your record would do to you. No one who has decent lending manners will take a second look at you.

When the most reputable lending institutions in the country don't think you are suitable for business, what options do you have left?

Everyone leaves you at the mercy of people who will take the most advantage of you - people who can charge you as much as 400% APR. These loan sharks will eat you alive and make your life miserable.

And so you wonder: Can I do anything to avert this situation? And are there ways I can avoid getting into this mess again in the future?

The short answer? Yes.

And that's the goal of this guide – to show you how to keep collecting agencies from destroying your credit. And on top of that, to show you ways to maintain a healthy score for the long haul.

Sounds appealing, right?

No, you won't have to play dirty tricks or pay considerable fees to some credit repair agency. Everything I suggest here falls under "Do It Yourself."

And, best of all, everything you do will be within the bounds of the law.

Having good credit can open all sorts of doors for you. A new life awaits you if you put the knowledge I provide into practice.

So, why are you waiting? Let's get started

Table of Contents

Chapter 1: Assessing The Damage

If you are a fan of the award-winning TV series Homeland, you probably love how Carrie Matheson and his mentor Saul Berenson love to look at the big picture.

Every time they hit a wall, their first instinct is to step back and take a bird's eye view of the situation. And all of a sudden, things get more precise.

Like that time when Carrie loses an asset to death. Completely broken, she runs to Saul, talking about how messed-up the espionage business is. They both ask questions that make them look at the situation from its origin. And it becomes clear who the murderer is and what their intentions for doing so were.

Or how about the seventh season when Carrie opens up to Saul about the unauthorized home surveillance she has been running on the President's Chief of Staff? Saul is disappointed at her behavior but still encourages her to look at the situation from another angle. She discovers that Dante, the FBI agent, has been playing her.

Both examples show the value of detaching from a situation and looking at it whole.

In the same way, it has come to your attention that your credit is in jeopardy, and you don't like the idea.

You probably want to throw a Hail Mary and immediately solve the situation. I beg you to reconsider.

When you do so, you'll solve your problem much more sensibly.

To use military language now is the time to conduct a hasty retreat and reexamine the situation to plan your next battle tactically.

Know Your Enemies

As you take a step back to look at the situation clearly, you should compile your list of enemies (your creditors) and the amount of money you owe them.

Yes, it might seem like a simple task (and a pointless one), but the reasons for doing it are significant, as we will see later.

Remember that knowing your enemies will keep you alert so no one attacks you from an angle where you don't see the blow coming.

You might wish to compile a list such as the one below:

Lender	Amount

Request To Receive Your Credit Reports

The credit industry teems with intelligent, crafty, and influential individuals.

At one point, they figured that the best way to determine someone's ability to pay their debts is to look at how they have behaved with debt in the past.

I know it doesn't sound fair to be judged by your past mistakes; after all, people do change. But that's how it is with these guys.

And so they keep a file of your borrowing history and bill payments with three of the most important credit bureaus – Transunion, Equifax, and Experian. And they've convinced the government that keeping and protecting this information is a good idea.

The file we are talking about, of course, is your credit report. Maybe you've heard of the name.

Each item on this file, whether positive or negative, holds some weight. And all that information is fed into a computerized mathematical formula (dubbed the name algorithm) that calculates your credit score.

So any chance you'll get at saving your credit score from getting any worse comes from requesting your credit report so you can see what lenders are saying about you and what you have done in the past.

Usually, you have to pay to get this information. But the government thought it fair to require the credit bureaus to give free access to it to every citizen once a year.

So, if you've never requested your credit report, now's the time to do it.

How to Request Your Credit Report

If you head over to Google and type in "download my credit report," you'll undoubtedly receive results from all sorts of websites claiming to give you access.

And so you might feel stuck. From whom should you request it? And how do you trust that they are a legitimate source?

And you are right to ask such questions.

Many of these websites will try to get you to pay for this access. Others might offer the report free but require you to opt into their email list. Before you know it, they are spamming you to death with various offers.

So here's the deal: there's only one source from where you should request your reports. And that's the official website at www.annualcreditreport.com.

I will not give you specific instructions on downloading your report because the website is self-explanatory and easy to use. Plus, the design might change when this book arrives in your hands.

However, what you need to keep in mind is to download reports from all three credit bureaus. The reports from these organizations keep track of the same information, with slight differences.

So if you want a proper glimpse of your credit situation, you must request all three. After all, the reports are free, so what do you have to lose?

Once you have the electronic reports on your computer's hard drive, it's time to dig through the information looking at essential items. The next chapter will cover what those items are.

Chapter 2: Collections vs. Charge-offs

Once you obtain your credit reports, it's time to review them, looking at what is on them.

Remember how I said negative items carry different weights in calculating your score?

Lenders look at one of the most important items: your history of paying bills. Have you always paid on time? Or have you made a habit of falling behind?

Most people don't know the importance of paying bills in good time. And if you are one of those people, change your ways today because diligence in paying your bills carries the most weight.

Let's digress for a moment and talk about what FICO - the most popular scoring model - takes into account while calculating your score. Five items go into the mix:

- Your history of paying bills
- The total amount you owe creditors
- How long you've been using credit

- Your history with new credit
- The types of debt you hold

To calculate your score, the Fair Isaac Corporation (the company that holds rights to the FICO algorithm) uses relative weighting of the above items. Here's how they represent the information visually:

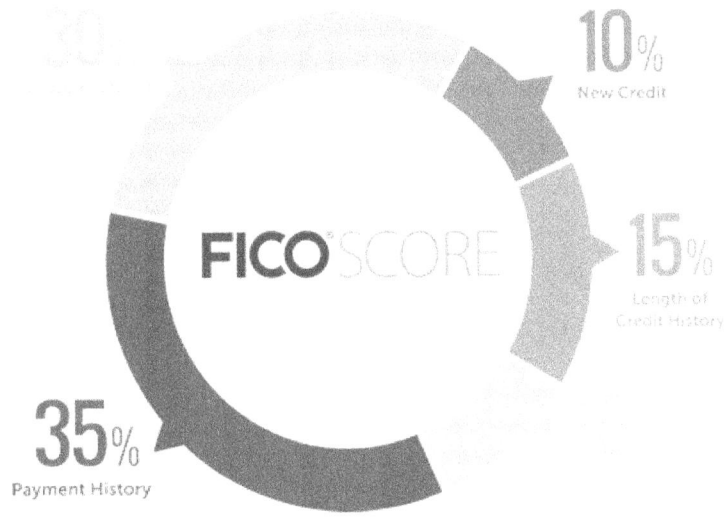

You can see that payment history takes up 35% of the overall pie. So, if you have no borrowing history, a reputable lender could give you a shot after reviewing your history of paying bills.

Most negative items on your report usually affect the payment history part of the equation. And the two most significant ones are collection accounts and charge-offs.

Let's look at each one of them in turn.

Collection Accounts

If you've heard the term collection account or seen it in your credit report, you may have wondered what it meant.

So here's how it goes.

Say you've borrowed from a card you obtained from Credit One. If you fail to pay after the first month, the company will try to contact you and get you to pay.

But you must understand that these companies must keep clean financial records. And at some point, having an unsettled account fails to make economic sense to them.

That means there's a threshold for them before they choose to give up on you and write off your debt as a loss.

Depending on the company policy, this threshold may last three to six months of non-payment.

And here's another thing: they'll treat your account similarly if you make payments below the required minimums.

So let's say it's been six months, and Credit One no longer believes you'll repay their debt. What do they do, then?

They may send it to an in-house collection team to try and recover the debt from you.

But many banks and lenders are not collection specialists. So this isn't the kind of business they prefer to conduct.

So Credit One opts for another choice: they sell the debt to some other party. That other party may be some debt buyer or a collection agency such as Sunrise Credit Services.

Whatever the case, your debt ceases to be with Credit One. Some other company assumes the responsibility of collecting money from you.

When debt collectors record your debt in their books, they report it to the credit bureaus.

And that, my friend, is how you end up with a collection account in your report. What follows are a series of calls from them trying to get you to pay up.

And what about the other item we discussed?

Charge-Offs

You can think of charge-offs as the original lender's way of getting back at you for not paying them their money.

You may think you can get away with it if you don't pay a lender back, and they give up and sell your debt to another party.

But the lender always has more power than you can imagine. They'll let you go, but they'll taint your image in the eyes of other lenders, so they know you are bad news.

And they do that by reporting your case to the credit bureaus as a charge-off. A charge-off means that they gave up trying to recover money from you. They essentially had to declare your arrangement with them as a loss.

And let me tell you, if your credit was once good, adding a charge-off on your report will make your score take a huge hit. The more stellar your credit once was, the more significant the impact will be.

And the worst part is that this kind of record doesn't go away until seven years have passed. That's how long you'll be paying for your mistakes. So I wasn't kidding about the kind of power a lender has over you.

But before you start thinking that your life is over, understand that the longer a negative item stays on your report, the more insignificant it starts to be. And most lenders refer to credit activity from the last two years. So there's a lot of hope for turning your situation around in the near future.

Collection accounts also stay on your report for seven years. But at least with those, you have room for negotiation, so you can make things better.

If you pay and pay well, you can convince a debt collector to have your record expunged. We'll look at how you can do that in the next chapter. But you must remember that you don't always have that kind of leeway with a lender who has reported a charge-off on you. Some may be willing to work it out with you, but many will not.

Anyway, debt collectors can be a real pain. So, in the next chapter, we'll look at how you can deal with them and keep them from making things worse for you.

Chapter 3: Dealing with Collection Agencies

Now let's deal with the big Kahuna.

So, there you are, going through your day as usual. Maybe you are hanging out with your friends and laughing your head off. Or perhaps you are having dinner with your family. And everything seems to be well in the world.

Then a call comes through. You can't recognize the number but can tell it is from an office line.

So you receive it only to hear a woman on the other end of the voice. "Hello, Sir. I'm calling from Citywide Credit Services." And then, she proceeds to talk about some debt you owe and that they are taking steps to collect on it.

You sit there, trying not to utter a word that would give away the nature of your conversation as everyone tries to act like there's nothing awkward at all.

Finally, you leave the table and head to the front-door porch.

After she briefs you on everything, you say, "I understand. We'll talk about this later."

You head back to whatever you were doing, but the question that keeps bugging your mind is: "My God, what do I do?"

This chapter will help you determine the proper course of action. So let's start with the first thing you should do:

Knowing Your Rights

Have you heard one of those cases where someone gets on the wrong side of the other only to get sued for millions of dollars?

I know. It happens every time.

A personal favorite is a bizarre story about a man who caught his wife cheating with a wealthy man. Of course, he couldn't do anything about her, but he did something unexpected to the loaded guy.

He sued the man for "alienation of affection." Who ever heard of such a thing? But he had the goods to prove his case, so he went after the guy. And he came out seven million dollars richer.

Crazy, I know.

And that's why it always helps to know your rights, for the world is full of crafty people who are out to take advantage of you if they can. And the way you protect yourself from falling for their traps is by knowing what is right under the rule of law.

Of course, your dealings with collection agencies are the best place to start.

Some rules govern how they should conduct themselves with you. And by making it clear to them that you are aware of what's right, you can stop them from making your life a disaster.

So what rules govern how collectors should go about their business? Here they are:

- They should not call you before 8 a.m. or after 9 p.m.

- They cannot call your boss or whoever is in charge of your place of employment

- You can instruct them always to call your lawyer

- They must not make any threats, such as those involving damage to your reputation

- They cannot threaten to seize your assets

- They cannot "talk dirty" to you on the phone

- They cannot misrepresent themselves and pretend to be someone else.

  Some lenders used to pose as law enforcement or some other official. But today, that type of activity is illegal.

- They cannot threaten to take you to jail

- They cannot talk to some other person, such as your spouse, child, or friend, about your debt. But they can speak to them about getting in touch with you.

- They cannot call you once you've made a formal request demanding that they stop

- They cannot call you more than seven times within seven consecutive days

Don't these sound like advantages with which you could live?

You bet. These rights give you some breathing room and allow you to live like an adult with dignity.

And that's precisely the way it should be.

Oh, and if new rights end up on this list, you can look them up on the Consumer Financial Protection Bureau website.

Now that you know your rights, it's time to do the next best thing:

Verify the Debt

Don't get into a habit of accepting everything a member of the credit fraternity loads over you. Always take your time to go over the details.

And in this case, you have an excellent reason for doing that.

A new set of regulations took effect on 30th November 2021. These rules stipulate that a debt collector should send you an official document notifying you of a debt you owe them within five days of them reaching out to you.

Without such an official notice, you can't even begin to discuss debt matters with them. Isn't that cool?

But here's where it gets even more interesting. Even if collectors do serve you with an official notice, you can still decline discussions about your debt if the notice isn't valid.

Do you know what that means? A valid Notice of Debt verifies that you are responsible for paying the debt. And without it, the debt is not collectible. So it would help if you always did everything possible to understand what makes for a valid Notice of Debt.

Even better, when a debt isn't verifiable, you can file a dispute with a credit bureau and take it down from your credit report. That's a chance to increase your score potentially.

Now, you may wonder why you should go through all the trouble to do all this.

Here's why: before the ruling in 2021, collectors would send Notices of Debt that didn't include some information items, and it would still be legal for them to collect the debt from you. That list is now updated.

So if your debt predates that period, and the collector buys it from a lender who doesn't supply all the accurate information needed, you might catch a lucky break that lets you remove the debt from your credit report.

Now that you understand what could be at stake if you don't verify that a Notice of Debt is valid, here are the pieces of information that must be present in it.

First, there's the matter of dates. The following dates must be present in the notice:

- The last date your creditor issued you with an invoice or statement regarding your debt

- The date when your creditor marked your debt to them as charged-off

- The date when you last made a payment to your creditor

- The date when you first made the transaction that led you to have this debt

- The date when a court made a judgment on the debt, in case your creditor sued you

And regarding the issue of courts, checking dates is crucial because it helps you determine whether the statute of limitations has expired on your debt.

You probably don't understand what that is yet. No worries, we'll look into it later.

Other essential items of information that must be present in your Notice of Debt include:

- The name and mailing address of the debt collector that is contacting you

- Your full name as well as mailing address

- Whether your debt was part of a particular financial product from the creditor

- The name of the original creditor

- The account number that held your debt

- The name of the creditor who currently demands payment from you

- The total amount you now owe, plus any payment history on the debt (including any extra charges such as fees, interest, etc.)

And here's another thing that must be present in the notice they send you: a statement advising you of your full rights under the Fair Debt Collection Practices Act to dispute the debt within thirty days of receiving the notification.

Also, the notice is incomplete if it doesn't come with a form allowing you to file your dispute right there and then, depending on your reason. The three reasons that enable you to dispute a debt are:

- You believe that the debt in question is not yours

- The amount indicated on the notice is not accurate

- Other reason(you'll need to explain)

Don't worry if all this sounds too much for you. When in doubt, consult the CFBP website. They have provided a sample Notice of Debt that should help you cross-check whether the one you received is valid.

And that brings me to the next point I wish to make.

Always File a Dispute

Any time you come across an incomplete Notice of Debt, you must take the chance to dispute it.

Doing so is vital because if you let the thirty-day window provided by the law close, you will not have the ability to dispute anything. The debt will automatically be yours, and you must pay it.

You need to understand that if your debt predates a couple of years, it's likely that the debt collector holding it purchased it before the November ruling of 2021.

And so they may have incomplete information about you or your debt in their files. Or maybe some of it got lost or misplaced as the files were in transit.

In any event, it's not unusual to find that the debt collector is having trouble collecting specific information about you from the original creditor.

And without you being the wiser, they can trick you into accepting the debt as yours. And even if the debt is yours, this is a legal matter, not a moral one. If they can't provide everything the law requires, you have the power to assume the debt is not collectible. Then you can convince the bureaus to remove it from your credit records.

Assuming you have found a reason to dispute the debt, you can send them a letter informing the collector of your decision. To do this, use the attached form on the Notice of Debt. But as you do so, confirm that the document complies with Regulation F (the November ruling).

As you highlight your objections in the letter, be sure to ask for the following as well:

1. Request that they send official documentation showing that you owe the debt. Asking for a copy of the original signed contract is a good idea.

2. Ask them whether the statute of limitations on the debt has expired. Many will be reluctant to give you an answer to this one. If they do, there's a good chance that it has passed, and you have a legal advantage over them.

3. Ask the collector to prove they have the legal authority to collect debts in your state. In other words, are they licensed to operate in your state? And if they are, ask them to provide a copy of the license so you can verify. (Remember, they are not legally allowed to lie about this stuff)

4. Ask that they provide you with a copy of the last billing statement they sent you.

The collector must respond to your request for verification within thirty days. If they don't, they can't collect money from you, and the law requires them not to report the debt to the bureaus.

How sweet!

And now, let's talk about something that a lot of people don't know about, and that leads them to take actions that land them in trouble unnecessarily.

Chapter 4: Statute Of Limitations

Has a debt collector contacted you to collect on a debt dating back a few years? If that's the case, a statute of limitations could save you from having to pay.

Earlier, I touched upon a term called the statute of limitations. I even advised you to ask if it had expired on your debt as you filed your dispute.

So what exactly is this thing?

It simply refers to the time during which parties involved in a potential conflict can take the matter to court to resolve it. Once this period elapses, the case can no longer hold up in court.

Now, the statute of limitations applies in many other areas. Still, it also applies to consumer debt because lenders and collection agencies usually have a predefined period during which they are legally allowed to collect a debt.

The thing with a statute of limitations is that it's not the same for all states. Each state defines how long it should last. But generally, it can last anywhere between three and six years.

That means it's up to you to check whether the statute of limitations on your debt has expired. Please find out the length of time in your state, and check it against the date since the debt was declared delinquent by the original creditor.

This detail is crucial because once the statute of limitations on your debt has expired, the creditor or debt collector cannot launch a lawsuit against you to recover the debt. That means they cannot garnish your wages or come after your assets to repay themselves.

And here's the part that gets people in trouble: any time you acknowledge a debt that has exceeded the date of the statute of limitations as yours, you risk resetting the clock on the whole thing.

And then you'll have granted the creditors and debt collectors the legal right to do all sorts of things to you, including suing you or placing a lien on your property.

Also, the debt goes back into the reports and stays there for years. Ouch!

That's why debt collectors always look to play all sorts of games to unsuspecting credit consumers. They may try to get you to make all kinds of legally binding commitments, such as asking you to make a small payment or sign some agreement forms so you can acknowledge the debt as yours. Please don't fall for the trap of accepting any deal with them.

Find out whether the statute of limitations has expired and then exercise your legal right not to have to do anything.

The Statute Of Limitations Doesn't Completely Let You off The Hook

Understanding what an expiry of a statute of limitations means for your debt situation is essential.

An expired statute of limitations only means a lender cannot legally collect your debt. But it doesn't take away their right to report the debt to the bureaus.

So, do not expect to remove one more item from your credit report just because you realize a statute of limitations has expired. It will not happen unless seven years have passed. And yes, your score will keep being affected in the meantime.

But like I said, the longer a negative item stays on your report, the lesser of an impact it gets to have on your score.

And remember, most lenders will look at your credit behavior over the past two years as a guide for lending.

So my advice, unless you have a guilty conscience that makes you want to do otherwise, is to hold off from taking any action on any debt that has passed its statute of limitations.

Chapter 5: Stop the Constant Calling

Once upon a time, collectors would blow up your phone with calls as much as fifteen times a day. And boy, were they annoying.

And it seems law-makers took notice too. Most folks think that guys in Washington may not have debts, but they are people like you and me.

I suppose that's why they capped the number of times a collector could call you. As I've already said, once a collector contacts you, they must wait another seven days before making another call.

Isn't that great?

And if that doesn't work for you, you can write to them, instructing them to contact you by email or text. The letter could even tell them not to reach you for whatever reason.

The way you accomplish this is by composing what is called a "stop contact" or "cease" letter. That'll do the trick.

And don't worry if you are stuck figuring out how to write one. You can find an excellent sample posted on the CFPB website to use as a guide.

However, you need to keep proof that you sent the letter. That's why you should make a point of sending it via certified mail. And as you do that, be sure to request a return receipt.

Once the collector receives your letter, they can notify you of the following action they'll take.

But I wouldn't worry if the statute of limitations has expired. You can call their bluff and have them go to court, knowing they wouldn't win the case anyway.

If you do, however, owe a legitimate and verifiable debt, they may choose to file a suit against you.

That's why it helps to know how to work things out with debt collectors.

Working It Out With the Collection Agency

So far, we've discussed what you can do when a debt collection agency cannot prove that you own the debt they are trying to collect.

But most of the time, you don't get that lucky. It may very well be that the debt is yours and they can collect on it.

Does that mean that everything is lost?

No, not even by a long shot.

You must start thinking like a business person willing to make a deal. The collection agency is in the business of earning a profit. They don't care about you or your dog. They will work with you if you make them a deal worth their while.

And that brings me to the next thing I wish to tell you.

People in the lending business have worked out the odds of different types of people paying back the money they owe. And they generally conclude that most people who remain delinquent until their accounts get charged off likely never repay their debts.

So what do you suppose lenders do when they are in this position?

Of course, they sell the debts off to a collector or some other debt buyer for whatever they can get. And in many cases, the debt collector receives a sweetheart deal – cents on the dollar.

According to an article by Motley Fool, collectors buy debts at an average rate of 4 cents on the dollar. In other words, a $1,000 debt could have easily cost them as little as $40. Unbelievable, right?

And here's the point I'm trying to make. Collectors can settle for less than a debt's face value. All you have to do is make them a deal that guarantees they'll earn a profit, and everyone's happy.

Doesn't that sound like hope? You don't have to pay everything you once owed. You can opt for less, and it'll still be okay.

And this revelation gives rise to another question: What kinds of offers are acceptable? How low are debt collectors willing to go?

An article by U.S. News gave away the goods on this issue. It turns out that many collectors will accept 40% to 60% of the owed balance if necessary.

So now we know that you could settle for less than half of what you owe. Incredible.

But I have an even better idea. How about you start negotiations for as little as 10% and see what happens?

Remember, these guys bought your debt for close to nothing. You could work out a pretty good deal for yourself by being smart.

A debt collector marks your debt to them on a credit report in four general statuses:

- Unpaid
- Settled for less than the original balance
- Paid in full
- Removed

When negotiating with a collector, you must be gunning for the last two statuses listed above. The more you are willing to pay, the more they will do for you. Also, your charm comes in handy, so bring it with you.

Having your record removed is the Holy Grail of all credit fixes. But you usually can't guarantee it. Paid in full, however, is achievable for most people. And if your report indicates "paid in full," the negative impact on your credit score is minimal. Some scoring models even ignore items listed that way.

But there's one thing you'll want to remember as you negotiate anything with a debt collector – always get a written agreement.

Do you wish to avoid being double-crossed? Because it can happen.

If so, make sure your arrangement with a debt collector is legally binding. And if they are sensible enough, there's no reason why they shouldn't go along with it.

A Word on lawsuits

It should go without saying that not all debt collectors are created equal. Some are very aggressive.

You might find yourself up against a collector who is out for blood. This collector will take you to court to recover even small amounts.

Don't worry about it. It's the debt collector's right.

But you shouldn't make the mistake of not showing up. Any time a collector sues you, lawyer up and appear in court.

Failing to attend court is one of the worst mistakes ever. The judge might decide to rule against you, which can mean grave consequences, such as garnishing your wages or seizing your assets.

I'm sure you wouldn't be happy to hear any of these things.

But the good thing is that if you follow what we have discussed in this chapter, there's a good chance you will not have to show up in court.

And now, let's talk about how you can maintain good credit once you've attained it.

Chapter 6: Good Credit Practices That Keep You In Shape

Losing good credit is a lot like losing a healthy weight.

Anyone who's been down the road will tell you how painful it can be once you wake up to the fact you are not keeping your ideal weight.

And that pain motivates you to start doing something about it. Maybe you start hitting the gym. Or, if you are busy like me, perhaps you work out at home after work.

Months go by, and you start seeing some progress. Before long, you are in good shape again, and everyone is begging you to tell them your secrets.

You feel proud, but deep down, only you know what kind of hell you had to go through to get here. And you are afraid of doing anything that will make you slip back and lose all that progress.

Similarly, once you have climbed out of the trenches and your credit is looking good again, you don't want to fall prey to the mistakes that put you there in the first place.

So let's talk about what you can do to ensure just that.

1. Pay Your Bills On Time

You probably grew up hearing that paying your bills on time was your responsibility once you became an adult.

Well, that rule remains as valid today as it ever was.

It turns out that even seemingly innocent stuff, such as failing to pay library fees or parking tickets, somehow makes it to your credit report. So don't compromise.

And if you are the type that tends to forget, it's a good idea to set up automatic payments. Ensure your automated system sorts everyone out at the right time and you are all good. With our advanced technology, doing that kind of thing is a no-brainer.

Remember, paying bills on time makes up 35% of your score. So, don't mess around.

2. Check Your CUR

CUR refers to your credit utilization ratio.

How much of your available credit do you always use? If Bank of America allows you $10,000 on their card, do you take all of it?

That's called maxing out; if that's what you are doing, you must stop—starting now.

Lenders keep tabs on how much of your available credit you tend to use. And if you are taking all the money on the table, you are sending a signal that things are not looking very well for you financially.

And that's just one more reason for them to distrust you. So they put a giant axe on your score, which you'll want to avoid.

Now, how much is a healthy utilization ratio?

Most experts agree that 30% is a decent maximum. But generally, lower is always better. You're golden if you can keep it as low as 10%.

3. Avoid Closing Out Old Lines Of Credit

Your history of credit use is another factor that explains a lot about you to creditors.

Someone who has been reliably using credit for a more extended period is a more trusted party than an overzealous new kid on the block with potential.

So, let me ask, do you have old lines of credit that you've been using for years? And are you starting to believe that debt is terrible and that you should close them out?

If that's the case, think again. Closing those lines will result in an immediate slump in your score because you'll have lost most of your record. It's like losing years of hard work at the push of a button. Please don't do it.

Let the cards stay. You can use them to pay for the basics at home, such as your Hulu subscription or cable TV.

4. Stay Away From New Credit You Don't Need

Your credit utilization ratio is a funny thing. Any time you open a new line of credit, you affect it negatively.

That's why you always need to keep your lines of credit as few as possible. That means turning down new offers of credit that you don't need.

Of course, lenders don't care about your financial well-being. Like everyone doing business, they want to reel you in to make the most dough out of you.

And they've devised crafty ways of doing that. They've even partnered with businesses. So when that cute clerk at the department store asks if you could accept a 10% savings if you sign up for their card, say no.

It may look attractive now, but you'll pay for it when your score takes a hit. Plus, having that line of credit makes it easier to splurge on things you never included in your budget (if you don't have a budget, don't do anything else before creating one right now).

In The Millionaire Next Door, the late Dr. Thomas J. Stanley profiled most American millionaire households as having only two credit cards– A Visa and a Master Card.

Think about it: most affluent households only hold two credit cards. Why should it be any different for you?

Two major credit cards are a good rule of thumb to follow. Limiting your number of cards to two will likely avoid most of the traps the credit fraternity sets for people out there. And your score will benefit from it.

5. Periodically Review Your Credit Reports.

You may be working hard to keep your record spotless, but that doesn't mean everyone shares in your spirit.

Creditors and bureaus may still be slipping errors into your report. So it would help if you kept a close eye to ensure they do everything right.

That means periodically ordering your reports to check that the information on them is accurate.

No need to overdo this. Once or twice a year is enough.

6. Rebuild Your Credit With Secured Debt

And what if you were being young and reckless and ruined a nearly perfect credit in the process?

You may be in a terrible spot, but that doesn't mean you should give up on yourself and your credit. The good news is that everyone gets a second chance at this game.

Also, remember how I said that most creditors examine your behavior over the last two years to make decisions?

You have a shot at making things right again in their eyes. And there are tools to help you with that.

I recommend starting with secured credit cards, which is a product that most creditors offer. They work like regular cards, except you put up a deposit first. This deposit is refundable any time you wish to close the account.

And so the creditor advances you funds to use. You make interest payments as usual and payments on the balance, which the lender reports to the bureaus. And over time, you rebuild your reputation as a reliable borrower.

Isn't that cool?

Do that for two years, and you are back in many lenders' good graces.

Conclusion

To sum it up, most of us never fully appreciate the importance of having a good credit score until we lose it.

And when we are in the dumps, it can be challenging to know how to navigate the terrain because we lack the appropriate information, and debt collectors are always scheming to take advantage of us.

But it turns out that building a damaged credit isn't hopeless once you know what to do. You can rely on the new rules drafted against the debt collection industry. You can also check whether your debt has exceeded the statute of limitations.

And if all fails, you can still negotiate with a debt collector for much less than you originally owed.

Doesn't that sound like hope?

So why keep sitting there? Go out there and do something about it.

www.ingramcontent.com/pod-product-compliance
Lightning Source LLC
Chambersburg PA
CBHW070750220526
45467CB00018B/1806